Walking the Road

Walking the Road

A play in one act

Dermot
Bolger

**NEW
ISLAND**

Walking the Road

First published 2007
by New Island
2 Brookside
Dundrum Road
Dublin 14
www.newisland.ie

ISBN 978-1-905494-89-7

British Library Cataloguing in Publication Data. A CIP catalogue record for
this book is available from the British Library.

Typeset by TypeIT, Dublin
Cover design by New Island
Printed in the UK by Athenaeum Press Ltd., Gateshead, Tyne & Wear

New Island received financial assistance from The Arts Council (An
Chomhairle Ealaíon), Dubiln, Ireland.

10 9 8 7 6 5 4 3 2 1

Walking the Road *by Dermot Bolger was first staged by the Axis Art Centre, in association with the In Flanders Fields Museum, Ieper, at the Axis Art Centre, Ballymun, Dublin, Ireland, on 5 June 2007 and at the Ieper Town Theatre, Vandenpeereboomplein, Ieper, Belgium on 16 June 2007.*

Cast
Frank: Colin O'Donoghue
Companion: Kelly Hickey

Production
Director: Ray Yeates

Produced by: Róisín McGarr
Set and costume designer: Marie Tierney
Lighting design: Conleth White
Sound and music: Mark O'Brien
Production assistants: Niamh Ní Chonchubhair
and Norma-Jean Kenny
Production manager: Paul Hyland
Stage manager: Marella Boschi

Cast
Frank
Companion – playing a multiplicity of roles, including **Frank** himself. This should ideally be played by a female actor, but may also be played by a male actor.

Time
A dreamlike continuum of time that swings between Rathfarnham and Slane at the start of the 20th century, Ieper in 1917, limbo and the present day.

The text was commissioned under the South Dublin County Council In Context 3 Public Art Commission Scheme, funded under the Department of Environment, Heritage and Local Government's and the National Roads Authority's Per Cent for Art schemes.

SOUTH DUBLIN COUNTY COUNCIL'S PER CENT FOR ART PROGRAMME 2008–2009

AN ROINN COMHSHAOIL, OIDHREACHTA AGUS RIALTAIS ÁITIÚIL
DEPARTMENT OF THE ENVIRONMENT, HERITAGE
AND LOCAL GOVERNMENT

Introduction
Sebastian Barry

For many years, for decades even, Dermot Bolger has been thinking and writing about the Irish poet Francis Ledwidge, who, as one of the thousands of Irish Nationalists in the First World War, was caught in the terrifying briars of that war and destroyed, leaving a whole life of poems unwritten. The war stopped many young lives in mid stride. Ledwidge was no exception, and this play marvellously captures that: the loss of girlfriend, friends, all the interrupted narrative of family life, and his progress as a poet.

As a publisher Dermot Bolger issued an edition of Ledwidge's poems (with an introduction by Seamus Heaney) some years ago, which was an act of friendly homage in itself. As a very young poet he wrote an intuitive and affectionate poem about Ledwidge, at a time when there was precious little interest in the First World War, much less those Irishmen who had gone out to fight in it, only to be more or less stymied in history by the events of 1916 and after.

So Bolger had an early affinity with the poet in Ledwidge. In the years since first thinking about him, he has developed himself a vast range in his own fiction and plays and poetry, in particular his recent masterly novel *The Family on Paradise Pier*, which ranges across the entire twentieth century. He has acquired, as one might say, the background and landscape looming tragically behind the lone figure of Ledwidge walking the country roads.

This is what gives his play such unexpected ease and

poise, and allows the language to speak with a gentle and subtle theatricality that is very rare. This play shows the fruits of long thinking about the fate of an anomalous man (whom Seamus Heaney has referred to as 'our enigma'). It is one thing to have an interest in a fine poet, and be intrigued and touched by his life. It is another to write a beautiful, floating, faithful play about him, as Dermot Bolger has done here.

The war of course produced many extraordinary poems, Tom Kettle's lovely 'To My Daughter Betty' for instance, and some of Ledwidge's own. Like Kettle, also a fervent Nationalist, he was thrown all out of kilter by the Rising at home, and wrote his famous elegy to Thomas McDonagh, one of the leaders of the rebels. But he wrote it in the army, looking back towards Ireland one can suppose with perplexity and wonder, and equally, a dreadful alarm for himself as an Irish person in a 'British' uniform. Neither he nor Kettle survived to test the temper of the new times that were coming for Ireland.

Dermot Bolger imagines Ledwidge eternally turned towards home. There are really affecting moments everywhere, none more so than the litany, towards the end of the play, of the lost souls of young fellas passing along the road, with their strangely vivid, ordinary Irish names. The war ended about ninety years ago and you cannot go to it because the roads don't lead there anymore. But Frank Ledwidge is trying to come home. He hardly knows who he is, or where home lies, but surely we can place a light for him now in the window. At any rate, Dermot Bolger offers him the solace of this beautiful play. It is a handshake and a welcome, which is all that a soldier or a poet asks.

Author's Note

At unlikely times I think of the poet Francis Ledwidge. Maybe when playing football with my sons or driving home, knowing my wife is asleep upstairs. These were the futures he missed, the mundane yet magical realities. Ledwidge never knew a son or wife. Fate tackled him from behind, just shy of his thirtieth birthday, when he was killed by a stray shell while helping to build a road behind the front line during the nightmare Third Battle of Ypres in Flanders. His shattered limbs were dumped in the bomb crater before the road building recommenced. His face became trapped inside a handful of photographs. Like other Great War poets, he looks out from those photos, condemned to the limbo of being forever young.

But like thousands of fellow Irishmen, he was also condemned to another limbo. Rupert Brooke's death immortalised him at home. It was the same for the Canadian poet John McCrea, whose poem 'In Flanders Fields' features on the Canadian $10 bill. Their posthumous reputation was simple, with no legacy of divided loyalties, no whispered rumours. The Britain to which poets like Siegfried Sassoon returned might nurse ambivalent feelings towards how 'great' that war was, but they were never viewed as traitors – they could publicly discuss their experiences. Their stories were not blotted from their country's collective memory. However, only in recent years is the Irish experience of the Great War being fully explored.

Ledwidge was born in 1887 in a labourer's cottage in Slane, County Meath (now preserved as a museum). His father was an agricultural labourer, a profession where you could slave into your eighties and still be called 'the boy'. Neighbours were clear about his mother's best course of action when her husband died when Francis was four, leaving her destitute. Francis and his three-month-old brother, Joe, should be placed in an orphanage while she tried to raise the older children at home. But Anne Ledwidge was determined to keep her sons at home by working all hours in the fields. Francis and, in time, Joe joined her after school as she slaved in the frosty earth, longing for dusk, when they could return to the cottage and there might finally be warmth and some food.

Ledwidge left school at fourteen to work in the fields. In 1907 he became a seasonal road worker, but was lured underground when a copper mine opened. Conditions were dire. Despite Ledwidge's youth, other workers asked him to present their demands for safer conditions. He did so, a union leader organising a strike three years before Jim Larkin organised the Dublin workers. But when Ledwidge presented their demands, his fellow workers capitulated, leaving him sacked as a troublemaker.

In between those jobs, he worked as a grocer's apprentice in Rathfarnham in Dublin, writing his first proper poem there and walking home through the night with nothing except the gift of verse.

A determined and active Nationalist, Ledwidge resigned from the Irish Volunteers in 1914 in protest at the recruiting call of their leader, John Redmond. But haunted by sightings of his love, Ellie Vaughey, with a new beau (called Dempsey in the play) and without even a steady job to show for his success as a poet, Ledwidge did what many people supporting Redmond shied away from. He decided that Europe's war was Ireland's war, and therefore his war, and enlisted in the Royal Inniskilling Fusiliers.

Even today, Ledwidge's reason for joining the British army rankles with many Irish people and is torturously debated. To accept that he enlisted – like 200,000 other Irishmen – not from any love of England but from a sense of duty to Ireland was a heresy against a consensus opinion which downplayed Irish involvement in that war.

But *Walking the Road* is only in part about Ledwidge. The Ledwidge within it is filtered through my own reimagining to hopefully become a sort of Everyman, a representative of the thousands of Irishmen who walked the same road as him, from the south Dublin villages of Rathfarnham, Tallaght, Lucan, Clondalkin and Saggart (many of whose dead are mentioned here), from my native village of Finglas and the nearby fields around Ballymun and indeed from every corner of Ireland. Hopefully in some way he also represents all the young men from every nation who died ninety years ago in that nightmare battle for Ypres. Every time a road is built in Ieper (as Ypres is now called), more bodies are still churned up, more autopsies held, more clues left for the In Flanders Fields Museum to piece together, using buttons and fragments of bone to try to identify the missing. Young men like the small crew of road builders blown to pieces that day in 1917 when men paused to drink scalding tea and turn their thoughts to home, to the secret places in their hearts to which they would never return.

I wish to thank Piet Chielans, director of the In Flanders Fields Museum, who instigated this project; my director, Ray Yeates, and everyone at the Axis Art Centre in Ballymun who have provided a platform where this and other of my theatrical works might be staged; Colin O'Donoghue and Kelly Hickey, who brilliantly inhabited these characters in the first production; and everyone involved in the South Dublin County Council In Context 3 Public Art Commission Scheme, under which this text was commissioned and completed.

Dermot Bolger
Dublin 2007

Walking the Road

All involved with *Walking the Road* would like to remember Carmen Gruwez (1954–2006), beloved wife of Piet Chielens, director of the In Flanders Fields Museum, Ieper

We begin in blackout. The stage starts to lighten, so that we make out two figures. **Frank** *is propped against a broken stile to stage left. He is motionless, eyes staring out lifelessly. In his late twenties, he wears a First World War uniform so faded that it is impossible to distinguish any features. The minimal set yields an abstract suggestion of unfocused landscape. There are two half-filled sacks of sand tied together with twine at the front of the stage and two thin pieces of wood lying to the side, which may be used to represent guns and bayonets. Other broken objects may be used to create something to sit on. At the back of the stage lies the seemingly lifeless figure of the* **Companion** – **Frank's** *constantly changing, and sometimes unseen, companion in this state between life and death. He is also in an indistinguishable uniform.* **Frank** *lifts his head stiffly as if waking, takes glasses from his pocket and puts them on.*

Frank No night should be this cold. No moon, the stars glinting like shrapnel. And no sense of where I am or who I am. I just know that I am walking home.

Companion (*softly, still lying down, watching* **Frank**) Such a long walk, Frank, such a long time you've been walking home.

Frank (*looks down*) This must have been a uniform once, if I could only remember what colour, what regiment, what reason we had to slaughter each other.

Companion You should be able to remember, Frank. Try.

Frank (*rises slowly*) I'm so cold, so numb, that something inside my body must surely ache – my guts or intestines. That's what they say happens when a bullet hits you, your body closes down into a state of shock where you feel no pain.

Companion But that's just a comforting lie, like eternity. Any man you ever saw get shot screamed, and the longer he lay in the open, the more he screamed.

The **Companion** *starts to crawl slowly towards* **Frank**, *until he is clutching onto his leg.*

Frank They screamed at you to finish them off as you passed, clutching at your legs while you scrambled in terror over the dead and the dying. They tried to grab the bayonet from your hands and finish the job themselves.

Companion (*pleads quietly*) Kill me, let me be done with this.

Frank Let me be done with life. Surely I had a life once where the sights of No Man's Land would have sickened my core. Once upon a time, but what time, what place?

As **Frank** *turns, the* **Companion** *rises, keeping a certain watchful distance between them.*

Companion (*softly prompting*) No night should be this cold. No moon, the stars glinting like shrapnel. You just know that you are walking home, Frank.

Frank (*removes his glasses and puts them in his coat pocket*)
Time to push on. I can't rest here. I need to push on, one step in front of the other. I pushed on through ninety miles of rain to Salonika once.

Companion Bayonet charges through the trees from maundering Bulgarians. Famished Serbs shivering and bewildered. Remember?

Frank I remember a girl there, feet blue with cold, her family scattered or slaughtered, her eyes so…

Companion (*kneeling, little girl's voice*) When will I know the taste of bread, Mama?

Frank If I'd had bread I would have given it to her. All I had were the empty pockets of my army great coat.

He removes his coat and places it around her shoulders.

Companion So you gave her your coat instead, remember?

Frank I wrapped it around her shoulders, because I knew what it felt like to yearn for bread as a famished child.

Companion (*little girl's voice*) When will I break my fast? When will I taste bread, Mama?

Frank Afterwards I didn't mind the rain or daily bayonet charges. I minded the fact that my coat pockets had not been empty – my reading glasses were still inside them.

Companion (*rises*) All the deaths you've seen, men mutilated and gassed…

Frank And yet I wept over the loss of a pair of reading glasses.

The **Companion** *circles him, breaking into in a mocking parody of a soldier marching.*

Companion (*sings softly*)
    And when the war is over what will the soldiers do?
    They'll be walking around with a leg and a half
    And the slackers will have two,
    So right away, so right away,
    So right away, Salonika, right away my soldier boy…

He stops marching and drops the coat, watching **Frank***, who has begun to march on the spot.*

Frank Our comrades in Salonika had given us up for dead, because nobody could survive walking that road. I marched into Salonika, legs like brittle sticks, my back so crippled with rheumatic arthritis I could barely stand upright. (*stops marching*) Eyes staring at us as if at a line of walking ghosts. And I knew that nobody back home, if I ever reach home, would understand this. (*confused, looks at*

Companion) Who are you again? Where did I say I was walking to...?

Companion You're walking home, Frank. It's time to push on.

Frank You can't just walk home from a war. If I don't rejoin my outfit, I'll be shot. Maybe I fell behind, unable to keep up in the dark. I've got to think straight and remember. Where was I last? Pilkem...Boezinghe...Ypres, with its moving rivers of mud, the smell of trench rot, cold terror...no night should be this cold...the stars like... (*alarmed*) Maybe I was on watch? They shoot soldiers who fall asleep on watch. It teaches you a lesson so you'll never do it again. The generals are proud of their record – no repeat offenders.

Companion (*quietly*) I'm the one on watch, Frank, watching over you.

Frank (*agitatedly*) Feels like I've been walking forever, but I started out from somewhere once. I had a family once, a name. I should have photographs – all soldiers have photographs. Grave-faced girls in their best frocks, passed along the trench by the lights of flares. Each man's whispered intake of breath.

Companion (*a whispering presence at his shoulder*) Remember Ellie, Frank? She just wanted something more.

Frank I can remember dozens of photographs, I just don't know if any belonged to my life.

He rubs his face softly as the **Companion** *slowly falls back as if shot dead.*

Frank I've hardened labourer's hands. My face feels almost boyish, but with several days' stubble. That's one thing I learned in this war, stubble grows for days on a corpse.

He turns to see the sprawled **Companion**, *who looks at him.*

Companion (*German accent*) Remember me, Frank? The foxhole in No Man's Land?

Frank I remember scared eyes that had finally ceased blinking. A soldier so young I could have sworn you hadn't started shaving.

Companion Downy fuzz on my chin was the only thing growing for half a mile on any side of us.

Frank You had photographs, I remember, a German dog tag. You were dead, but at least you knew who you were.

Frank *turns, agitatedly searching his pockets as the* **Companion** *rises to stand behind him.*

Frank I'm going mad, talking to myself. Amnesia, that's the medical term. Military tribunals have their own term – desertion. They cure amnesia with a bullet – especially if you're Irish. (*pauses*) Am I Irish?

Companion If so, then what are you doing here, Frank?

The **Companion** *tosses* **Frank** *one of the long pieces of wood.* **Frank** *kneels beside the two sand bags, as it working with the piece of wood.*

Frank In Ireland, I built roads. I'm only a lad, but I work with grown men at a crossroads where barely a cart passes. Cows flicking flies away with their tails, surveying us from a rich farmer's land. Not my land; I possess no land. Fields are like women...

Frank and **Companion** ...only for looking at and longing for.

Companion (*as road worker*) Give over your chat, boy, and brew us some tea in that billycan. Make it thick enough that we can race a fat mouse across it.

Frank (*drawn into scenario*) We've no milk.

Companion (*as road worker*) Haven't you warm hands and a winning way with cows? Hop into that field, Frankie boy, stare into her eyes and say, 'Sure, Gertie, a wee squeeze never hurt anyone.' If you're this shy with four-legged females (*leans over* **Frank**), God knows what you're like when they only have two. Go on, boy, I'm parched, my throat dry as death...

The **Companion** *suddenly rolls over as if dead and lies utterly still.*

Frank (*rises*) My throat dry as death. (*he drags the* **Companion** *towards the back of the stage, as if clearing corpses in a war zone*) I remember building another road, a road along mud so thick that you couldn't race a fat mouse across it. A mouse would sink like I watched wounded men sink, with only their arms waving, then no longer waving as they slurped from sight. What lunatic builds a road across mud? No foundations except the bones of the dead. We're laying planks across mud, with everything sinking, stretching away to eternity.

Companion (*rises to his knees*) When was that, Frank?

Frank I don't want to remember.

Companion We'll be here all night if you don't remember.

Frank I want to remember building roads in Ireland, shovelling stones down lanes and working on highways awash with steaming tar.

Companion That wasn't where you last smelled tar.

Companion *crouches like a terrified, beaten girl.*

Frank A girl I saw in a retaken French village. Head shaved, tar and feathers on her body. Disloyalty. Betrayal. Retribution. She reminded me of someone I once loved.

Companion (*more watchful*) Who?

Frank (*annoyed*) I feel like I've been hypnotised, like you're dragging me through time for sport. Who are you?

Companion (*kneels up in a position of pious prayer, boy's voice*) 'Oh, angel of God, my guardian dear.'

Frank What?

Companion (*boy's voice*) 'To whom God's love commits me here.' What's next, Frank, teach me what's next in the prayer.

Frank (*kneels beside him, gentle voice*) I've taught you before.

Companion Teach me again.

Frank 'Ever this day be at my side...'

Frank and **Companion** '...to light and guard, to rule and guide.'

Frank (*rises, moving forward*) From the time I could walk, my hands have been hardened by work. Fields in winter. Turnips to thin, potatoes to be picked amid the muck. And a woman waving to us. (*behind him, the* **Companion** *has risen to mime stooping to pick potatoes*) Our cottage empty, the grate cold, no food after we finish school, but this is not her fault. It is for our sake that she stoops in these darkening fields, hands raw with cold in the churned up mud.

Companion (*straightens up to call excitedly as* **Frank's** *younger brother, Joe*) There is Mama, Frank, I'll race you to her.

Both run excitedly across the stage.

Frank Mama! I'm running with my kid brother Joe through rows of withering stalks almost as high as us.

Companion (*as Joe*) Mama! Too excited to feel famished because we're calling her name and slowly she straightens up her jaded limbs, hands pressed against her aching back.

Frank Scolding us for coming, yet glad to see us, because we're such good little workers, in our bare feet and ragged jumpers. Little Joe jigging about so much that I don't know if it's from the cold or because he needs to wee. (*both sink to their knees, miming energetically picking potatoes*) But we laugh together as we sink to our knees. Three pairs of hands rooting through the muck before the frost congeals it into corrugated iron.

Companion (*as Joe, playfully pushing* **Frank**) The sooner we finish, the sooner we can turn for home. Isn't that right, Frank?

Frank (*playfully pushing him back*) That's right, Joe. The road dark and our cottage unlit. But soon we'll be inside with lamplight and a fire and fresh bread from the oven, soft with butter.

Companion (*as Joe*) Will there be enough bread, Frank?

Frank Enough to appease the hunger always inside us like a guardian angel, enough to think that God hasn't forgotten us again.

Companion (*as Joe, lying down to stretch out for sleep*) Then ghost stories and Mama's songs will make us forget how the bedroom is so cold.

Frank (*still kneeling beside the sleeping* **Companion**) The bedroom where we watched our eldest brother die. The blanket is thin with an old coat thrown over it, but Joe's body is warm as I spoon into him. He's asleep within seconds and I know that he'd walk through fire for me because he's the best kid brother in the world.

Companion (*sits up*) And Frank is the best big brother who would mind me anywhere, even if Mama had sent us into an orphanage like the neighbours had urged her, saying that we'd surely starve to death here after Daddy died.

Frank Mama never sent us away, even when our eldest brother, Patrick, came home from his job in the city coughing up blood.

Frank *lies back as if racked by coughing.*

Companion (*crying, covering his ears*) I can't sleep, Frank, with the sound of Patrick coughing, his struggle for every gasp of breath. (*he rises*) I can't sleep, Frank, with all the sounds…

Frank (*rises*) …of bailiffs banging at our door, policemen sent to assist with our eviction. Patrick's rasping cough saved us – the bailiffs too scared of catching his illness to carry him out on his mattress from the cottage.

Companion (*as Joe, scared, low voice*) Are the bailiffs gone, Frank? I'm so cold, hiding here in the garden. Who are the men blocking the road?

Frank They're neighbours, Joe. The neighbours who'll pay for Patrick's pine crate to be lowered into Daddy's grave. The wind howling that day and how empty the cottage seems without Patrick's cough.

Companion (*as Joe, excited*) Come out to the yard, Frank. Mama is making a bonfire of Patrick's mattress.

Frank That night, an old mattress appeared on our doorstep, all three of us too exhausted to hear the cart stopping or know who brought it. Next morning, Mama dragged it into the house.

Companion (*as Mother, dragging the two sandbags across the stage*) You two boys will sleep on this. I've lost one son, I'll not lose two more to any orphanage. We'll live or starve, but we'll live or starve together.

Frank Mama kept us at home because we belonged with her. That's why I love to lie awake, spooned into Joe's body in the dark, listening to him breathing and knowing that Mama is sitting up by the dying fire, mending for neighbours, with barely enough light for her to see by.

Companion (*older now, observant*) Maybe she doesn't need to see any more, Frank. Maybe this late hour is when she finally sleeps, her hands automatically stitching away by themselves to earn a few more pence with which to push us out into the world.

Frank Where was I? This unearthly silence has me rattled. So long since I've known silence. Always there's mortar fire, and if the guns go silent, the other noises are worse. The screams of the unsaveable, the not-yet-dead caught in a barbed wire limbo with a letter of condolence already dispatched to their wives.

Companion You knew a silence like this once before, Frank. You are walking the forty-two miles home from

Rathfarnham through the night. You are sixteen years of age…

Frank …and scared to face my mother after all her scheming to find me a job in Dublin out of the fields and the rain.

Companion (*coming close*) But you loved the fields and the rain.

Frank *grabs the* **Companion** *in a friendly headlock as they swagger downstage, cocksure, brimming with vitality and mischief.*

Frank Donning long trousers at fourteen to bring in a farm boy's wage, free to walk the roads with Joe of an evening. Rarely a coin in our pockets and barely an arse in our trousers.

Companion (*as Joe, released from headlock*) Walking for miles, just to burn off energy.

Frank Charging down slopes by the Boyne, pretending that posses of Zulus were chasing us on horseback. (*looks at* **Companion**) Do Zulus ride horses, Joe? (*jumping about*)

Companion (*as Joe*) They do in our games, Frank.

Side by side, they move forward with the walk of gunslingers.

Frank They do when we're roaming the vast American prairies, driving some farmer's cows down a lane choked of cow shite and dandelions...

Companion (*as Joe*) ...and behind us we can hear hordes of wolves and aborigines and red coats and Zulus...

Both pull imaginary guns and fire off several high-tempo rounds.

Frank ...and Apache and Blackfoot and Cherokee and Navajo and rebel Boers from South Africa screaming in Dutch and tripping over their long red beards...

More rounds of imaginary gunfire to punctuate the line.

Companion (*as Joe*) ...and they being chased by Roscommon bogmen in their hairy pelts...

Yet more rounds of rapid gunfire to punctuate the line.

Frank And behind them, Dublin society girls in red garters running barefoot, wanting to commit terrible sins with our bodies. (*pauses, aware of Joe looking perplexed at him*) Not that Joe and me would have known a society girl or, indeed, a garter from an alligator...

Companion (*as Joe*) ...except that both would likely snap the fingers off you if you went near them.

Frank But even though I love my brother Joe, he could swing left at the crossroads to lure away the bogmen and aborigines and Zulus and I'd swing right to let the society girls chase after me into the woods. I'd strip naked, knowing that they were peering out from among the trees, and I'd dive into the green water, startling kingfishers and herons. Not a pick of fat on my young body, only muscle from labouring in the fields.

Companion (*as Joe*) You've gone quiet, Frank.

Frank Joe's voice bringing me back to earth amid the cow shite and dandelions and swaying rumps of cows lumbering ahead of us. (*swings an imaginary stick and roars*) Get away into that field. Holllaa! Hiiighupp, you brute of a heifer. (*quieter*) Close that gate, Joe, and we're finally done.

Companion (*as Joe*) Will I race you home? Just give me a head start, because you're older and too damned fast.

Frank (*furtively taking a slip of paper from his pocket*) I'll show you something first.

Companion (*as Joe*) Is it something you found up above on the road? One of those drawings of girls in corsets?

Frank No, something I wrote.

Companion (*takes the sheet of paper from him and stares at it, puzzled*) What class of yoke is that?

Frank It's a class of a poem.

Companion (*as Joe*) And you say you didn't find it up above on the road? Did you copy it from a book, then?

Frank I told you, Joe, I wrote it. They're my words.

Companion (*as Joe*) They don't sound like your words. If you wrote it yourself, how do you know it's a poem? Who told you it was one?

Frank Doesn't it look like one?

Companion (*as Joe*) Sure, I wouldn't know a poem if it bit me on the backside, Frank.

Frank (*deflated, taking it back and tearing it up*) You're honest at least, saying to my face what people would say behind my back.

Companion (*as Joe, upset*) What did you tear it up for?

Frank It was only bloody nonsense.

Companion (*as Joe*) It wasn't nonsense. It was bloody marvellous, like a picture made with words. You could be famous, Frank, have your words printed in *The Drogheda Independent*.

Frank Don't be daft.

Companion (*as Joe*) You're daft tearing it up. Did you show it to Mama?

Frank I'll show her a poem if I ever get one right.

Companion (*as Joe*) How will you know it's right?

Frank I just will, you daft sod. Now I'll give you a head start to that blackthorn tree, then race you home.

The **Companion** *runs eagerly towards the back of the stage, then stays there, facing away from the audience.* **Frank** *goes to follow, then stops, distracted, deflated.*

Frank How many miles is it home? I could have sworn that I knew who I was a moment ago – I knew my name, rank and number. I could have sworn that I had a brother here with me. Such silence, like the whole world is holding its breath. No noise except… (*turns, startled*) …the beat of woodcock wings. There amid the trees, the glimpse of a kingfisher, a coloured spurt of blurred wings. I know where I am now. I'm here to meet a girl in the woods by the Boyne. I'm praying Ellie will come, even if only to say that she's leaving me. All I possess are words wheras her family possesses land. Land marries land, but she says that my poems are like magic, carrying them on her bicycle into *The Drogheda Independent*, where they're printed as curios between the local marriages and deaths. If my poems have any magic, it's because Ellie's white skin and laughter fills every line. (*his hands are outstretched,* *as if mesmerised*) I can see her now through the trees with her back to me. When I put my hands over her eyes, she'll laugh and say...

The **Companion** *turns suddenly, blowing a shrill whistle. He adopts an aggressive stance and a Cockney accent. At the whistle,* **Frank** *falls and crawls, terrified, towards the side of the stage, covering his head for protection.*

Companion (*as sergeant*) Get your bloody head down, man! Bloody Irish! Think you're beside a frigging river? (*the* **Companion** *has also begun to crawl across the stage towards* **Frank**, *who is almost inaudibly whimpering with fright*) We're up to our necks in a river of mud, where the only fish are rats who'll gnaw through your boots while you sleep. Listen to our guns flattening those German bastards. When we go over the top at dawn, Paddy, the Huns will be crying out for their mammies. The only white skin you'll find in Flanders is German flesh to drive a bayonet through.

Frank (*scared*) The woods are gone, Ellie gone. There's just the stench of mud and decayed flesh. How could I have thought the shells exploding overhead were stars? Too dark to see the faces of men fixing bayonets around me. (*by now the* **Companion** *is lying on top of him, almost in an embrace*) My dream was so real that I can still feel my hands about to cover Ellie's face. Don't walk away from me in the woods, Ellie, don't steal my peace of mind, don't torment... (*he manages to stand up*) I want to wake up! So scared to have to leave this trench and run through that blasted wire. Every time I black out into sleep, I dream about the smell of mustard gas. Mustard.

The **Companion** *has risen and stands back from* **Frank**, *singing almost to himself.*

Companion (*as jovial Meath farmer*)
    The rich man in his castle,
    The poor man at his gate,
    God made then high or lowly
    And ordered their estate.

Frank That mysterious substance which rich folk ate when I was a boy, that Ellie's people used to decorate the side of their plates.

Companion (*sits as jovial farmer*) You're holding that horse long enough, Frankie lad. Climb up beside me and away back to the farm.

Frank (*picking up the sand bags and settling himself beside him*) Yes, Master.

Companion (*as jovial farmer*) I'll not be your master much longer. They say your mother has a grand position arranged for you in Rathfarnham, in the county of Dublin. A grocer's apprentice, no less. You'll be too posh to talk to any of us.

Frank I'd be scared of Dublin, Master.

Companion (*as jovial farmer*) You're a good lad – a bit odd, scribbling away at the table at night – but you'll be fine once you know your place. (*resumes his tuneless hymn*)
  All things bright and beautiful,
  All creatures great and small...
(*he flicks an imaginary whip*) Giddy up, the slowest horse in creation.

Frank The horse is tired, after the two hours we stood outside the pub waiting for the master. A sack of provisions is open behind us, a jar falls out: mustard.

Companion (*laughs as jovial farmer*) One swab of hot mustard up that horse's backside and we'd fly home at speed, lad.

The **Companion** *moves off, leaving* **Frank** *alone.*

Frank Darkness under the whispering branches arching above the road. A fox motionless in the ditch. The master sleeps beside me, the horse lifting his tail. I unscrew the jar silently, place a finger to my lips, then want to spit the mustard back out. That's how money must taste like, I think, bitter and yellow and burning. (*he crosses the stage and dumps the sand bags down at his feet as he sits*) How long ago was that? Another lifetime, yet those fields still call to me. I see a robin on a broken stump and he sings to me of home. I see a sunset above a Flanders trench and imagine a skyline of horse chestnut. When was it – last week, last year, a lifetime ago? – that we paused by a cluster of trees during a lull in the shelling? Dangerous to venture in there, where mines could be planted. But a blackbird sang from their depths and every note transported me back to when I mended roads and knew nothing of nerve gas or amputations. A billycan boiling in a ditch, an upturned bicycle wheel spinning lazily.

Companion (*calls out as Cockney sergeant*) Lance Corporal Ledwidge?

Frank How could that same blackbird have followed me into this war? How could he sing those same notes amid the few trees left standing? I ventured into the trees, where a rat bolted from the undergrowth.

Companion (*as Cockney sergeant, annoyed*) Lance Corporal Ledwidge?

Frank Startled, he dropped something at my feet, then retreated a few paces. It was half a hand – a thumb and two gnawed fingers. Were the fingers German or French, English or Irish? Had they once stroked a girl's cheek like I stroked Ellie's cheek on the night when I failed to win her? The night when I longed to kiss her and say, 'You mean more to me than life. I have no land, but I have prospects. My poems are being published in a London magazine. They call me a peasant, but they pay six shillings a line.' I failed to win Ellie because I was a coward and this rat knows that I'm still a coward, too sickened to pick up the half-chewed hand.

Companion (*as Cockney sergeant*) Lance Corporal, come out from those trees or I'll do you for desertion!

Frank The blackbird stopped singing. I flung a rock at the rat, who dodged it. It looked like he was smirking, like half of Slane had once smirked about me. (*he rises*) Six shillings a line in London, yet no work in Ireland except labouring on the road. What could I do? The rat would dig up the hand no matter how deep a hole I scraped with my knife. I heard the click of rifles, my unit moving on. I knelt to pray for whomever once owned those fingers, whatever age or nationality or religion. Because we're all trapped here like insects under glass.

Companion (*as Cockney sergeant*) Frank, for God's sake, come out. (*more exasperated than annoyed*) Bloody poets!

Frank I emerged and said nothing to my sergeant, because what was there to say? We marched on in formation, but I walked alone. (*he closes his eyes*) I closed my eyes to drown out the rattle of guns across the scarred landscape and in my mind I was once again leaving the village of Rathfarnham in the dark. I was sixteen years old and terrified, but I knew that I was walking home.

Companion Such a long walk, Frank, but you'll be there by dawn. Joe will have woken, sensing something strange. He'll be standing out on the road, waiting for you to come.

Frank (*opens his eyes*) Mama's great plan to get me out of the fields that stole away her middle years. We barely possessed the train fare to Dublin. (*he stalks across the stage, followed by the* **Companion**) From there, a long walk up into the mountains to Rathfarnham. Following the road past Harold's Cross with signs for Templeogue and Tallaght. A farm boy pointing out the Hell Fire Club where rakes once chased girls in garters and played cards with the Devil. Then the bridge over the Dodder, the Yellow House pub, the constabulary barracks and (*stops*) my own devil waiting in the doorway of the Rathfarnham House.

Companion (*self-importantly, chest out*) W.T. Daly, Esquire. Proprietor of these premises, licensed to sell spirits, fine wines and stout. Beyond this curtain, ladies may enter to purchase household provisions. We deliver to the quality in their fine houses at Beauford and Bloomfield and Fairbrook, to the Farrens in Knocklyon House and the Rogers family at Acrebrook. And we don't refuse the pennies of the poor in Kelly's Cottages. Can you ride a bicycle, boy?

Frank Yes, Sir.

Companion (*self-importantly*) Good, because you start making deliveries this evening. Firstly to Whitechurch

Vicarage – you'll know it by the lime tree in the garden.
Then up winding lanes in Ballyroan and Ballyboden,
where a camel would struggle and even the sheep get
nosebleeds and vertigo. So, chip chop like a Chinaman,
stack them shelves, pack this lady's bag and smile.

Frank (*staggers under the weight of imaginary tasks, then
kneels at the sand bags as if they were sacks of provisions*) Mr
Daly's backside would be the envy of any Meath cow.
Tightly imprisoned in shiny britches but only dying to
escape. If a short-sighted bull passed through
Rathfarnham when Mr Daly was bending in his shop
window, he'd have had something more urgent to
complain about and make his eyes water.

Companion (*as grocer, self-importantly*) What did you say,
boy?

Frank Nothing, Sir.

Companion (*as grocer, self-importantly*) Nothing comes
from nothing. That's Shakespeare. Do you read, boy?

Frank Yes, Sir, any books I can find.

Companion (*as grocer, self-importantly*) I don't approve of
shop boys reading, it might give them notions. Unless
lives of the saints, although perhaps maybe not...too
many bad examples of charity. Still, you can write?

Frank Yes, Sir. I love to write—

Companion (*as grocer, interrupting*) And I love to see my boys writing. Write down the price of everything, boy, because everything has its price. Sugar, cinnamon, snuff, sheep drench, carbolic soap. Write the prices down and memorise them. Know your prices and know your place and you'll know everything there is to know about the world. Now sweep the floor before the last of God's free daylight is gone.

Frank For five nights I climbed Daly's stairs to an attic bed.

Companion (*as Joe*) It feels so lonely here in the bed without you, Frank.

Frank Joe's voice, Mama's voice, every bend of the road home calling out to me. (*moves away from the sacks*) I fought against homesickness because I was now a grocer's apprentice, learning to understand the world's limits by writing down the price of snuff and sheep drench and carbolic soap. But on that fifth night, words spilled from my head into lines of verse. Words beyond the horizon of W.T. Daly, Esquire. Words with a power stirred by my longing for home. It will break Mama's heart if I return empty handed except for a few lines of verse. But the words conjure up home so vividly that it feels like I am already there. I creep down the back staircase of Daly's emporium, past chests of Indian tea, rows of drawers for spices, boots hanging from the ceiling.

Frank *crosses to the edge of the stage and proceeds to walk slowly around its very extremities during the next changes.*

Companion You close the door and stand in the darkness of Rathfarnham village with the gaslights turned off. Behind you, the dark shapes of mountains. Ahead of you, the haze of distant lights from Dublin city.

Frank No night ever felt this cold. No moon, the stars glinting like shrapnel.

Companion You cross the Dodder unnoticed, the night quiet as the land of the dead. To your left, the parish of Tallaght in the barony of Uppercross. Before you, the village of Templeogue. If you were a blackbird, you would see all the isolated townlands with barely a light shining. Old Bawn with its paper mills; Jobstown's teeming streams; Balrothery Hill and the Greenhills; the quietude of Chieverstown and Fortunestown and Fox and Geese Common amid the darkness that stretches towards Lucan and Clondalkin and Saggart.

Frank *(stops)* And no sense of who I am or where I am, I just know that I'm walking home.

Companion Past paper mills and flour mills and remote dispensaries. Into Harold's Cross and along deserted streets until you reach the city of the dead at Glasnevin cemetery. Here the road dips to Finglas Bridge. To your right, the fields of Ballygall and Balbutcher stretch away to Santry and Coolock.

Frank I climb the main street of Finglas village. Ahead of me, the darkness stretches to Ashbourne and Slane. I am beyond tiredness. I just keep walking, carrying the uncertain gift of this first true poem. Will I be there by daybreak?

Companion There and back again, Sir.

Frank So why should I be scared of the darkness when my whole life stretches ahead? I am not scared because I know that when I finally arrive, Joe will be standing out on the road in the dawn.

Companion (*as Joe, confused*) It's the queerest thing, but I could have sworn Frank was coming home.

Frank (*to* **Companion**, *who seems unable to see him*) Joe, I'm here, I'm home at last. Joe, can you not see me...?

The **Companion** *circles him for a tense moment, with* **Frank** *anxious and disorientated.*

Companion (*as Joe, sounding slightly older*) Sure, I wouldn't recognise you, Frank.

Frank Why?

Companion (*as Joe*) You're so scrubbed up. Hurry now or you'll be late. If you polish them boots again, you'll have no boots left.

Frank Where am I going?

Companion (*as Joe, amused*) You're going to dine in a castle, man. Who'd have thought that a few old poems in a copybook would open such doors? (*he takes* **Frank's** *hands and spins him around in great circles*) Away with you now on your next journey through life.

Frank (*turning*) Yes, I do remember. I recall a headlong rush of years. A decade of toil spins past since that night I walked home from Rathfarnham as a boy. Sacked at twenty for leading a strike in a flooded copper mine. Stooping in farmers' fields, then finding work labouring on the roads.

Companion (*as Joe, circling him*) And all that time the poems keep coming, printed locally in *The Drogheda Independent*. Think, Frank, try to remember where you are.

Frank Ellie's white skin lighting up every verse. (*tries to stop turning*) Ellie, where are you? What place is this that I'm trapped in?

Companion (*as Joe, circling him*) You're outside Lord Dunsany's castle, Frank, twenty miles and yet a million miles away from our cottage. You're ringing the bell at the great door to which the postman delivered your copybook of poems.

Frank *stops turning as at the* **Companion** *steps back.*

Frank I remember the tilt of the butler's nose, ready to direct me to the tradesman's door before his Lordship appeared in the vast hall.

Companion (*as Lord Dunsany, steps forward to shake his head*) I have looked for a poet from among the Irish peasants because it seems to me that only among you is there in daily use a diction worthy of poetry. From this day on, Frank, regard my library as your library, think of us as fellow writers, as neighbours and colleagues.

Frank I want to read every book here by you and by all the other Irish writers too.

Companion (*as Lord Dunsany*) And I'll ensure that you meet them too, and, just as importantly, that the world discovers you and your remarkable poems.

Frank (*steps back*) I remember thinking I had found a world where what counted was the words I possessed and not the possessions I lacked. His Lordship introducing me to people who rarely noticed my type, the type who mend their roads and wash their clothes. Half of Slane mocking me for trying to be something I wasn't; for cycling into Dublin in a bow tie to visit the literati in their salons, passing around press cuttings from their American speaking tours. Clairvoyants who could commune with the dead but not with the poor. I perched with one buttock on their sofas but it didn't make me belong as they queued to shake hands with his Lordship's protégé, to feel connected with the dirt under my scrubbed fingernails by meeting a road worker. Their butlers frisked me with their eyes on my way out. Then the long cycle home. Mother never truly closing her eyes until she heard the latch on the door. Joe waking in the small room we shared.

Companion (*as Joe*) I left out your working clothes on the chair. What was it like, Frank? Did you read them a few poems about us?

Frank (*to Joe*) I did, Joe, now go back asleep. (*to himself*) But there was little about our poverty in my poems. Nothing about tunnelling for copper on bruised knees aching in a flooded mineshaft. Nothing about hauling rocks to fill potholes in the teaming rain. The lexicon of what earned six shillings a line in London held no room for our lives. They wanted spider-peopled wells, with the poor hidden away behind honeysuckle and woodbine.

Companion (*as Lord Dunsany*) Use my library at your will, Frank, but I may not be back until Christmas.

Frank Where are you going, your Lordship?

Companion (*as Lord Dunsany*) War broke out this morning, Frank. I've enlisted. They made me a captain.

Frank A war between Britain and Germany is not
Ireland's war. Our struggle is for the right to rule
ourselves. It's what I've always agitated for. We won't win
that in Belgium or France.

Companion (*as Lord Dunsany*) You stay here and fight
your battle, Frank, but I need to fight mine abroad. I have
different loyalties, a duty to two lands. Don't try and
follow me, because war and poets never mix. I thought I
saw you yesterday walking with Ellie near my estate. I
stopped the carriage, but she was with some other man.

Frank (*turns*) Who owned no more land than me.
Dempsey. A common labourer, but with more spunk, not
flouncing around pretending to be someone he wasn't. A
man who didn't spend his life making speeches against
the war at the Navan Board of Guardians, to which I'd
been elected to represent the common man.

Companion (*as shopkeeper*) And they don't come more
common than this road worker lecturing us about
Ireland's right to be free. If the pro–German traitor loves
freedom, he can show it by fighting for other small
nations, like Catholic Belgium. But for all his Socialist
talk, this coward seems better with *limp* poems than *stiff*
resolve.

Frank Innuendoes, whispers and taunts. Saturday night
in the Conyngham Arms in Slane, the gramophone
blaring full tilt. (*calls to* **Companion** *as Joe*) Wind up that

record again, Joe, and get in another round of drinks, I need to go outside to shake hands with the unemployed. (*voice more sober, turns to face the audience, miming the actions of urinating*) The back wall of the unlit yard, a row of men shaking hands with the unemployed, each aiming to leave a streak of piss on the stonework higher than the last man. Cigarette smoke, stale alcohol, a thump of hobnailed boots across the cobbles. (*the* **Companion** *walks over to stand beside him and also begins to mime the action of unbuttoning his fly and urinating*) A broad-shouldered confident presence in the line beside me. Dempsey.

Companion (*as Dempsey, quietly*) Isn't it shocking to be unemployed, eh, lads?

Frank An old farmhand beside Dempsey winking.

By slightly adjusting the countryman's cap that he is wearing and by crouching to suggest a far more wizened man, the **Companion** *effortlessly slips between being Dempsey and being the old farmhand also urinating on the other side of* **Frank**.

Companion (*as old farmhand*) Isn't it a good thing that at least someone here has work to do, Dempsey, eh? In like a brave lion, eh, then out like a baby lamb.

Frank I didn't look up, my hand shaking. Dempsey's voice remained quiet.

Companion (*as Dempsey*) That class of talk is uncalled for now, John-Joe, out of order.

Frank My piss straying until it sprinkled Dempsey's boots. I wanted him to hit me so I'd have an excuse to hit him back in that unlit yard. He was bigger but I didn't care. He could punch me senseless once I got one chance to rearrange his features.

Companion (*as Dempsey, deadpan*) Don't worry about splashing my boots, Frank. I'm sure someone I know would lick them clean.

Frank Dempsey turning away, unruffled, shaking himself dry.

Companion (*as old farmhand, doing up his fly*) Put that brute of yours back in your trousers, Dempsey. You must find them fierce tight. Did I ever tell you, Frank, what old Mrs Finnegan, the midwife, says and she delivering young Dempsey? (*woman's voice*) 'Mother of God, but it's a boy for sure and his grandfather must have been a racehorse.'

Frank I wanted Dempsey to make some coarse reply. I begged God that he might push me or give me any excuse to swing my fist. But he just winked to the grinning men and walked away.

Companion (*as Dempsey, unflappable, confidently self-contained, moving off*) You're out of order, John-Joe, right out of order. Besides, the midwife didn't mention no racehorse. The term she used was a stallion.

Frank I stood in that dark yard with my fly undone, pretending to keep pissing though nothing would come. Because I knew that when I re-entered that pub, every drinker there would have a smirk.

Companion (*as sly local drinker*) Pouncing about like a Dublin dandy, yet he can't keep his hands on a girl. (*impersonates* **Frank**) 'I've no land.' (*own voice*) The only land Dempsey owns is lodged in his trousers, though it's a fair stretch, they say, with good drainage.

Frank (*turns slowly*) 'The poems are grand, Frank,' Ellie said, that last night in the woods, 'but I want something more. I'm not an ornament.' (*shouts roughly, as if re-entering the bar*) Who changed the bloody gramophone record? Can't a man take a piss without some fool changing the record?

Companion (*as local drinker*) We're sick of the same bloody record, Frank. You don't own the gramophone. It's not a family heirloom your mother used to wind up in your cottage.

Frank (*furious*) Mention my mother again and I'll stretch a line of you across that floor with my fists.

Companion (*as local drinker*) Would that be a six-shilling line?

Frank *swings a fist and the* **Companion** *ducks, swinging* **Frank** *around to pin his arms behind him. He shoves* **Frank** *downstage.* **Frank** *falls to his knees.*

Frank Ructions and the publican barring me, claiming I was astray in the head. Joe found me hunched down under the arches of the bridge. (*looks up at the* **Companion**) It's too small, Joe, don't you understand?

Companion (*as Joe, kneeling beside him*) What's too small, Frank?

Frank My life in this goldfish bowl of a place. I thought that poetry would earn me respect, Joe, but all I earn here is mockery. Every man has a label for me: pro-German, coward, traitor, failed lover. I've no hope of a job except mending roads. I'm sick of the smell of asphalt and drinking tea from a scalding billycan in the rain. They laughed at me in *The Drogheda Independent* when I turned up, looking for a reporter's job. 'Sure, you're the poet of the roads, Frank,' they said. 'Readers love to think of you writing poems out in the ditches. Stick to what you know.' (*he rises*) Know my place, they meant. There's no place for me here except on the roads. I'm going up to Dublin, Joe; I'm going to enlist.

Companion (*as Joe, rises, shocked*) Are you mad? You said that no Irishman should enlist. You came to blows with people here over it. Let the imperialists fight their war, you said. Our battle for an Irish parliament won't be won in the trenches in Belgium.

Frank No, but I'm starting to think that it might be lost there. I'm no Briton, but if the only way to fight an enemy common to both our civilisations is to wear their uniform, then I'll not have people say that while Britain defended us, we just sat on our arses and passed resolutions.

Companion (*as Joe*) But Frank, after all your talk...

Frank Can't you see, Joe? All anyone in Ireland does is talk and pass resolutions. All I did with Ellie was talk, and see where that got me. She took me for a coward, without an acre of land or a stir in my hand to chance my luck.

Companion (*as Joe*) Going to war won't win Ellie back, Frank.

Frank I'm not trying to win her back, Joe; I'm trying to forget her.

Frank *walks away in a loop that brings him back to centre stage.*

Frank The world had an awful lot of forgetting to do, because half the young men in Dublin were queuing up in that barracks. Queuing to forget or queuing to find work or blindly following their pals. They were queuing up too in Glasgow and Cardiff and Birmingham, in Hamburg and Dusseldorf and cities I'd never heard of. Recruiting sergeants herding men into line.

The **Companion** *picks up one of the long pieces of wood and tosses it to* **Frank**.

Companion (*as cajoling recruiting sergeant*) Hurry on, lads, or the war will be over before you've time to be part of it. Quick or you'll miss your chance to strut about, impressing the girls in your shiny boots. Don't come crying to me when the fun is over before Christmas.

Frank We were going to war like it was a football match. Being paid seven shillings a week, a shilling more than a line of poetry in London magazines. But I was finished with words. I grabbed the bayonet they handed me and twisted it through the guts of a sack of rags. Maybe the Dublin lads saw the faces of Germans, but I saw other faces as I plunged in that bayonet.

Companion (*as cajoling recruiting sergeant*) Dempsey with his hands on parts of Ellie you never dared imagine, boy: stick the blade into his guts!

Frank *takes several steps forward, using the wood as a bayonet, violently miming the action of plunging it into a sack with a scream, then retreating and repeating it again on the punch-line spur of each successive line.*

Companion (*as cajoling recruiting sergeant*) Faces of mine owners, faces of farmers with stingy wages: into their ribs, boy! The face of W.T. Daly, grocer and vintner of Rathfarnham, and all the grocers and vintners on the Navan Board of Guardians who called you a coward: twist the steel into their bellies; watch their mockery change to fear. Do you see any of them here, despite their talk about duty? No, they're safe behind their shop tills jingling out hymns of profit. (*alarmed*) Enough, man, stop!

Frank But I couldn't stop because the face I kept seeing in that shredded sack was my own face haunting me.

Frank *stands still, shivering, holding the bayonet.*

Companion (*as Lord Dunsany*) Frank? Is that you, Frank? What the hell are you doing here? I told you not to enlist.

Frank I've a mind of my own, your Lordship.

Companion (*as Lord Dunsany*) Your hands were made to write poems, not kill people. Remember that.

Frank I will, your Lordship.

Companion (*as Cockney sergeant, circles him*) He will in his arse and poems my arse. It's bayonets on, lads! Charge!

Frank (*moving forward again, holding out the 'bayonet'*) We charged through cheering crowds on the Dublin quays. We charged up the beaches at Suvla Bay into the teeth of Turkish guns at Gallipoli. We crouched in crumbling holes in the sand and rose and charged and then retreated amid the slaughtered bodies. We charged and charged as the battlefronts changed. What never changed were our screams during each bayonet charge.

Companion (*as Cockney sergeant*) Into their guts, men!

Frank Bayonets getting tangled in the ribs of dying men. Lads tugging, amid the spew of guts, to retrieve their rifle and run on through the mud, terrified and terrifying, inhuman and yet all too human. One continuous scream emanating from our throats as the dying flashed past and two years flashed past.

Frank *lowers the 'bayonet' and sits wearily.*

Companion (*as Cockney sergeant*) Corporal Ledwidge, you have post. Looks like this yoke travelled halfway around the world.

Frank *catches the small parcel that the* **Companion** *produces from behind his back and throws to him.* **Frank** *opens it and finds a small book inside.*

Frank I'd sworn to finish with poems during the war,
but the poems were not finished with me. Waking at
strange hours to scribble down verses.

Companion (*faintly, almost inaudibly, over his words*)
    This is the song a robin sang,
    This morning on a broken tree,
    It was about the little fields
    That call across the world to me

Frank On starvation rations in Serbia, a tattered parcel
reaches me. *Songs of the Fields* – my first book at last.
Containing the poem written above Mr Daly's shop. How
far away home seemed that night in Rathfarnham, when
I thought I understood homesickness. But a road had led
home from Rathfarnham. A night without stars, but I'd
known I was walking home. There is no road home from
Serbia. I read that childhood poem again while around
me men quietly freeze. No sound except a soldier
crippled with frostbite. (*shivers, distracted*) The curse of God
on such coldness; just give me a scrap of paper to keep
me warm. My head crippled with thoughts, filled with
ghosts.

Companion (*as Ellie's ghost*) I just wanted something
more, Frank. I was not an ornament.

Frank You're not dead, Ellie. You live on in scraps of
poems lost in trenches, caught on barbed wire, too
saturated with rain to be legible.

Companion (*as Ellie's ghost*) You know that I'm dead, Frank. I married hastily and died in the agony of childbirth, exiled in England years ago.

Frank I don't know. I don't want to know. I only have to close my eyes for you to haunt me. (*he rises*) Look, I open them again and find myself amid this row of silent men waiting for the dawn attack, eyes expressionless in the flash of shellfire, rain splattering against the rim of steel helmets. I see my comrades all around me, yet when I turn my head, they're gone. (*confused, distressed, letting the book fall*) Joe? Ellie? I don't like this place where I am, I can't remember how I came to be here. I only remember that we were building a road; we paused for scalding tea. The rain torrential; mud churning into liquid that sucked in the wounded. All of Flanders was aflame, all of Pilkem and Boezinghe and Ypres and Langemark and Poelkapelle. We were building a road amid the screams of dying and drowning men. We paused for tea and then…I don't remember…don't want to remember…I keep trying to forget. Why am I here alone in this purgatory?

Companion (*as Ellie's ghost*) You're not alone, Frank.

Frank Then why can't I see you, Ellie? Is this No Man's Land or the Promised Land? Why am I standing here so long, trapped in the eternity of one second? I can't go forward, yet I can't go home. I'm twenty-nine years old; I'm nineteen, I'm nine. I'm continually walking back through time, seeking that moment when I'll feel safe,

when I'll glimpse a fading sky between withering stalks
and the woman who will cure my hunger.

Companion (*as Ellie's ghost*) You know how long you're
here, Frank.

Frank I cannot measure time any more, Ellie. I'm half-
blind. At first I thought it was from the smoke of guns,
from the mist through which soldiers rise from trenches
to be slaughtered.

Companion (*as Ellie's ghost*) That isn't what blinds you.

Frank I'm blinded because my eyes remain mortal even
in death. If I could fully let go of the world of the living,
I would be able to see my companions cross these
Flanders fields, seeking their road home. But I cannot see
the dead, I only sense them brush past and pass through
me. Close your eyes and feel them brush against you like
the faintest cobweb: the dead who love you whispering
your name. Others whisper names that no living being
remembers. Names of dead girls who whisper back,
trapped in shoals of floating souls.

Frank *picks up the wooden 'bayonet' again and the*
Companion *picks up the second piece of wood. Holding them*
as weapons, they retreat warily to the very back of the stage.

Companion The thousands of young men who
shivered in trenches on the Passchendaele Ridge, who

crouched in dugouts at Messines, who longed to flee as they waited for a captain's whistle.

Frank Who followed each other up mud-caked ladders, with an officer's bullet awaiting any man who turned back.

Companion (*sings softly, child's voice*)
Three blind mice,
Three blind mice,
See how they run,
See how they run,
They all run up to the farmer's wife,
Who chopped off their tails with a carving knife.
Did you ever see such a thing in your life...?

Frank *joins in the slow and creepy rendition of this nursery rhyme; however, he is always half a line behind. As they sing, both begin to crawl forward, rising and then falling onto their haunches and stomachs again, as if passing beneath barbed wire and through mud. The effect is almost like witnessing the jerky movements produced by strobe lightning. By the song's end they reach the front of the stage, with* **Frank** *sitting to cradle the* **Companion's** *head on his lap.*

Frank Hear the whispers of men whose bodies were never found. I was a blind mouse tussled up in a grain sack, scurrying about with no way in and no way out.

Companion I wanted someone to hold me amid the bullets and screaming.

Frank I want someone to find my remains – a splintered skull and some buttons, two rows of teeth biting into a rusted identity tag.

Companion (*rises*) Feel them pass, Frank? Another shoal of souls from Ypres, another flock of swallows searching for Africa. Always at the end, one confused soul is struggling to keep up, clinging onto the past, unable to accept that it's simply too cold to stay here. It's time you took flight too, Frank, time to try and walk this road home again.

Frank I don't know how. I'm still just not ready.

Companion Think of one night, Frank. One night when you knew you were truly walking home.

Frank Creeping down the back stairs of Mr Daly's shop, crossing the main street of Rathfarnham village, walking through the dark of south Dublin. (*he rises and starts to walk around the extremities of the stage*) I carry my first poem close to my breast and I'm walking home. Will I be there by daybreak?

Companion We'll all be there by daylight. There and back again, Sir.

Frank (*approaches* **Companion**, *as they are both facing each other, centre stage*) For ninety years now I have been walking home. My name is Wolfgang and I am walking home. My name is Hans and Gunter and Gabriel...

Companion (*overlapping with him*) My name is Alasdair and Alexander and Dirk and Dieter.

Frank My name is Frederick and Flavio and Fritz and Felix.

Companion My name is Jan and Jonas and Jasper and Jammet.

Frank *and the* **Companion** *turn to face the audience, side by side.*

Frank My name is forgotten by every living being. I have lost my legs and arms.

Companion The mustard gas in my lungs still burns, even though my lungs were eaten by worms.

Frank I am the unremembered great uncle whose features you inherit.

Companion I live on in my laugh that only you possess.

Frank (*moves forward*) During lovemaking I am reincarnated inside your sharp intake of breath.

Companion You are not walking home alone, Frank.

Frank No, I sense thousands walking, a great host in tattered uniforms. Who are you? Why are you following me?

Companion (*moves forward to stop alongside* **Frank**) I'm not following you, Frank, I'm Edmond Chomley Lambert Farran, my body missing in the Ypres Salient. I'm walking to Knocklyon House, Templeogue. This is Hastings Killingley beside me, aged twenty-one, of the Vicarage, Whitechurch, Rathfarnham. Remember the lime tree in his garden?

Frank And I'm Joseph Whelan of Whitechurch Road, Rathfarnham. With James O'Toole of Templeogue and James O'Neill of Rathfarnham, and John and Patrick Nolan of Saggart and Willie Nolan of Lucan and Willie Nolan of Clondalkin too.

Companion Alexander McCann here, Frank, walking to Larkfield Cottages, Crumlin, with William McCormack walking to Early Cottage in Tandy's Lane in Lucan and Simon Scully of Newtown Cottages in Tallaght. And Robert Kemp of Rathfarnham and Thomas Kearns of Rathcoole.

Frank And Patrick Emmett here, with my son and namesake, both of us having fallen, both keeping you company as far as Finglas village, with John McDonagh, whose mother's house is on the Green.

Companion A fellow poet here, Frank Tom Kettle, walking with you beyond Finglas, turning for St Margaret's out the Ashbourne road.

Both move away from each other in a loop that will bring them back together.

Frank But I'll be with you as far as Slane itself – Frank Joseph Lynch here – we shared many a night's drinking.

Companion And we shared a name, Frank, though we never met. Francis Ledwidge, from Thomas Street in Dublin. I died, aged seventeen, in the Royal Dublin Fusiliers.

Frank And Michael Ledwidge here of Francis Street, Dublin. I died aged eighteen years.

Companion Thomas Clarke here, Frank, aged twenty-four, from Castleknock. Willie Pearse, aged twenty, of the Yorkshire Regiment, and Fr Willie Doyle, Jesuit, I died near you at Ypres.

They are back, facing the audience, side by side.

Frank And make room for the other Doyles: Joe Doyle of Tallaght, Joe Doyle of Wheatfield in Clondalkin, Patrick Doyle of Rathfarnham, Robert Doyle of Clondalkin, James Downes of Ballinsacorney above Rathfarnham – remember how the hills would break a camel's heart – and my neighbour Joe Cullen, from Ballyboden.

Companion And John Dillon of Kelly's Cottages, Rathfarnham, sharing your road. And Herbert Victor Wyon of Lucan who died three days after you in Flanders, Frank.

Frank We died on the same day and in the same battle, Frank. Richard Rodgers here, of Acrebrook in Rathfarnham, with my brother George, who died a few months later.

Companion And your friend and fellow poet, Thomas McDonagh, walking towards St Edna's in Rathfarnham, divided by uniforms, united by dreams. And Willie Pearse beside me, faithful like younger brothers are.

Frank And George Harbourne and George Griffith here, Frank, both Finglas men, with George Attley of Rathcoole – we call him George the Third. Stop pushing, lads, we'll all be home by dawn.

Companion And Patrick O'Callaghan walking to St Bridget's Cottages, Clondalkin and Michael Foley walking to St Patrick's Cottages, Rathfarnham.

Frank (*breaks away to stand alone*) And John Bell of Finglas. I was barely more than a child. I got confused, shell-shocked, near Poperinge in Flanders. I started walking, thinking I was walking home. They put me against a wall and shot me at dawn.

Companion (*a gentle hand on* **Frank's** *shoulder to draw him back in*) We'll be leaving you at Finglas, Frank Thomas Fowler and Richard Russell, cutting across the fields of Ballymun to Santry, with Thomas Kenny and Laurence Keegan walking on to Coolock.

Frank And James Moore here with them, walking to my birthplace of Abbeville House in Kinsealy.

Companion And James Connor leaving you now, Frank, heading for Old Bawn with the other Tallaght lads – James Collins and John Clarke and Joseph Byrne and Thomas Burke and…

Frank (*pleads, with his hands over ears*) Stop! Stop this whispering. (*looks up at* **Companion**) Answer me, do these men ever reach home?

Companion Not from any lacking of trying, Frank, because every night some last few, stragglers like you, still walk this road. But you must forget all those others now and forget everything, so that you can start on your own journey again. This time, I promise you, we can reach the end.

Frank Wait, I know your face, I…

Companion Of course you know me. Now come on, say the words… (*prompting him, firmly but gently*) No night should be this cold…

Frank …no moon, the stars glinting like shrapnel. And no sense of who I am. (*he looks down, lost, having forgotten the* **Companion**) This must have been a uniform once, if I could only remember. How long have I been resting? Time to push on. Where was it that I said I was walking to? On the tip of my tongue…my tongue so parched. (*he turns, alarmed, suddenly aware again of the* **Companion**, *who passes him and stands, centre stage, his back to the audience.*) Halt there! I said, halt! Are you deaf? I'll blow your brains out, man. (*softer, surprised, standing in front of the* **Companion**, *who has become* **Frank's** *younger self*) But you're not a man; you're only a boy. Can you not see me, boy? (*beat*) I know your face. Sweet Christ, I am haunted by it, because it cannot imagine the horrors that lie ahead. Such a long walk since leaving Rathfarnham. But you've reached Finglas. Ahead of you is the long straight road that will bring you to Slane before dawn.

Companion

I walk the old frequented ways
That wind about the tangled braes,
I live again the sunny days
'Ere I the city knew.

Frank Look at your young face. Was I really so innocent as this? Lying awake in that Rathfarnham attic where Mama sent me to avoid slaving in winter fields. Weighing out half pounds of Indian tea and cycling with deliveries to Knocklyon House and Whitechurch Vicarage. A boy in long trousers, determined not to cave in to homesickness. But as the verses spilled out, I felt like a soaring bird, able to see rabbits zigzag through the fields at every bend of the road home. Rise up and face the dark, face. You are afraid now to face your mother, but one day you'll have to face bodies being blown asunder. You will see love torn from you. You will wake in flooded trenches, having dreamed of home. This first poem will lead to others and make you never truly fit in anywhere again. You will be pinned down in the baked Gallipoli sands, freeze in Serbia, be hospitalised in Egypt and then, with your body crippled, be packed off again to Flanders as cheap meat for the slaughter. That's where your poem will lead, lad. But even if you knew all this, you would still walk this road for the magic feel of writing those lines.

The **Companion** *blows softly into* **Frank's** *face and turns to face the audience.* **Frank** *steps back and blinks, bewildered, unable to see the* **Companion** *or remember where he is.*

Frank Who was I talking to? Can't remember. I must be shell-shocked. I seem to have been walking forever, but I know where I am now: the main street of Slane, with my head reeling and me having never written to tell a soul how I was being shipped home on leave. (*sees the* **Companion**) There's Joe in the window of O'Neill's grocers. What a night we'll have, Joe. We'll visit Matty McGoona and sit on the stone seat in his orchard. I had new poems to read you, but I lost them on my walk. I'm just so glad to be home when I never thought to see Slane again after all my bad dreams and premonitions.

Companion (*as Joe*) Frank? Frank? (*confused*) I must be going daft, Mrs O'Neill. I could have sworn I saw Frank pass by your window just now in his uniform.

Frank (*desperate*) Joe, I'm standing right in front of you.

Companion (*as Joe*) Maybe I imagined it, or maybe he's come home on leave and never told any of us.

Frank This is a cruel time to be playing tricks on me, Joe.

Companion (*as Joe, perplexed, walks away*) I could have sworn it was him…I'll walk out to the cottage, just in case, and maybe I'll see him along the way.

Frank (*follows, then stops*) You won't see me, Joe, because I'm dead. Such a simple thing, yet such a hard thing to accept. But I'll walk with you some of the way. I remember everything now. I was building another bloody road. A battle raging for Ypres but we were safe for once, a mile from the front, watching scared men being marched forward and scarred cripples being carried back. No time to do anything except bury the dead where they fell. We were laying planks across thick mud in a thunderstorm and I said, 'Down your shovels, lads, there's tea coming.' Next thing I was flying through the air, gazing down at men below gathered round my shattered limbs. A stray shell, impossible to know who fired it. I should have felt grief, Joe, but I just felt sorry for the poor sods with a road to finish. Then I was soaring up, warm air beneath my feathers. And I wasn't alone. Our father was there and our brother Patrick and Ellie and the faces of men from Australia and Belfast and Antwerp and Berlin drawing me towards them. And the landscape below was covered by a confetti of words as I rose. All the poems I'll never write, all my evaporating words fluttering out of sight. (*he looks at the* **Companion**) I don't know why I'm telling you this, Joe, when you can't hear a single word I say.

Companion (*as Joe*) Sure, I'm listening to every word, Frank.

Frank But I'm a ghost, Joe.

Companion (*as Joe*) And what do you think I am, after ninety-odd years? Who do you think has been keeping you company all this night? Will we catch up with him?

Frank Who?

Companion (*as Joe*) Your young self walking home from Rathfarnham. Look, he's after reaching the last bend before home. Is he getting smaller or is that just the evening light? No uniform now or shop boy's trousers, just bare legs and bare soles.

Frank How old am I? I can't tell any more. Our cottage looks so dark after this long walk.

Companion (*as Joe*) But at least I'm beside you, Frank, even if we're shivering in the dusk.

They embrace and begin to move excitedly towards the back of the stage.

Frank Come on so, little brother, let's help her finish her work.

Companion (*as very young Joe*) Why did God take away Dada and Patrick, Frank? Why did the neighbours tell Mama to put us in a home?

Frank This is our home, Joe. Mama would never send us away.

Companion (*as Joe*) Can you see her, Frank?

Frank I can. There in that field. Come on, Joe, the faster we run, the sooner we reach her. The fire is unlit and I'm hungry and cold and I'm running to find you, Mama.

Frank *runs forward and falls onto his knees.*

Companion (*as Joe*) The earth is buckled into ridges of frost beneath our bare soles and we're so cold, Mama, that our flesh is turning blue.

Frank And this field spreads out into infinity, with frost laying siege to everything. Your stooped back is the only thing moving across the hardening earth, your face grey as stone, your lips colourless. I'm cold, Mama, and Daddy is dead and my soles are sore from the stones in the lane. But Joe and I have gathered sticks to light a fire once the work is finished. And I want to piss only it feels like there's shards of ice inside me and Joe keeps jigging too because he's only seven. But we'll soon help you to finish these potato drills. The way you smile, the way your face lights up when you see us, so that I no longer even feel the stones cutting my feet.

Companion (*as the mother, softly*) Francis, Francis.

The light begins to close in around him.

Frank And the way you call my name. My throat so parched, but you will find me water. And bread, warm from the oven and soft with melting butter. It's so long since I've eaten, but I'll know the taste of bread when Joe and I reach you, when the work is finally done, when we all walk home together through the dark. When the fire in our cottage is lit, Mama, and I can finally know the taste of bread.

Blackout

Born in Finglas in North Dublin, Ireland in 1959, Dermot Bolger has worked as a factory hand, library assistant and publisher. His nine novels include *The Journey Home, The Valparaiso Voyage* and most recently *The Family on Paradise Pier*. His debut play, *The Lament for Arthur Cleary* (1989), received The Samuel Beckett Award and his first play for Axis, *From These Green Heights,* received the *Irish Times*/ESB Award for Best Irish Play of 2004. He has been Playwright in Association with the Abbey Theatre in Dublin, Writer Fellow in Trinity College, Writer in Residence with South Dublin County Council and is currently one of the resident artists in the South Dublin County Council In Context 3 Public Art Commission Scheme.

In 1992, Bolger edited *The Selected Poems of Francis Ledwidge*, which was introduced by Seamus Heaney, and in 1998 he was invited, along with the poet's nephew, Joseph Ledwidge, to unveil a monument in Flanders on the spot where Francis Ledwidge was killed and where a tricolour now flies. In 2007 he edited a new edition of Ledwidge's selected poems entitled *The Ledwidge Treasury*.

Knocklyon House in Knocklyon, South Dublin County, was the family home of a First World War soldier who died in the Ypres Salient in 1917 and whose body was never recovered. Today the house is used as the Rutland Centre for Addiction. His name is among the real life names mentioned in *Walking the Road*, consisting of men from the Rathfarnham and Finglas areas and from other places through which Ledwidge passed.